CW00370293

Poetry Virgins -
and the divine co

Julia was doing a p

Newcastle, (the firs

performances), anc

It was a poem abo

through that experience, were in a state of virginity, or

that at least. We were all certainly new to group poetry
readings.

"So what shall we call ourselves ?" we wondered over Marmite
on toast and red wine at Julia's kitchen table.

"Well we've never done it before, so I suppose we're poetry
virgins....."

So the Poetry Virgins were born, immaculately.

Five years and several performances later the Poetry Virgins are
still here.

The name may have lost us some potential bookings. Religious
organisations may have been be threatened, however none of
us are called Mary, and we have done several gigs in church
halls and the Catholic Chaplaincy.

We have performed in many places and to many people where
poetry is not usually heard. In pubs and health projects, outdoor
festivals and television studios, (well Tyne Tees anyway), at
conferences and functions, (although curiously never at a
wedding), to women and to mixed audiences. Luckily most of
them seem to enjoy hearing things reflected in words: politics,
love, laundry, periods, pushchairs and shagging. We certainly
enjoy the lengthy discussions over the subject matter of a newly
written piece, usually still over red wine and occasionally with
toasted tea cakes.

The performances are accompanied by bits of paper, although
these days we have progressed to rather smart black clip files.
And Virgins have come and gone, mostly on to better things,
certainly more lucrative. We have appeared in the paper
("Heads together and smile please girls"), six Virginal babies
have been born (not in stables) and we are finally able to claim
a press release and a photograph album, and now an anthology.
So these days we are still called the Poetry Virgins but, having
done it hundreds of times in front of many people, we are now
just a bunch of old poetry pro's.

                                                    Kay Hepplewhite

Foreword

We have a strange relationship with poetry. Most of us did it at school and a lot of our enjoyment was knocked out of us by the red biro and blue pencil approach. Ho, Bill Shakespeare, seven out of ten for that sonnet, lad. Too many metaphors. Then there is the 'even a child of five can do it' attitude: I always get the kiddies to do Haiku: it's short and easy, only three lines. No matter that the Japanese masters of Haiku studied and meditated for decades to perfect their art.

School fed us Byron, Shelley and Keats, but out of class, my generation lapped up the new generation of poets. Well, you didn't have to make it scan or rhyme.

You
didn't have to
make it
rhyme
to make it.

Now it seems a bit dated, like slang. But what goes around, comes around and we'd learnt something: here were people like us writing about life that we knew, ordinary things, stuck in a bus queue, hopelessly in love, knocked out by the beauty of a tree. Poetry jumped off it's lonely peak in Darien and into paperback and it was ours. Pub basements and upper rooms started holding readings, amazed by the thirst of the poetic muse. Real ale and writing too ?

In the sixties The Barrow Poets bought poetry into the streets by simply photocopying their own poems and selling them from a barrow. Performances, books and even LP's (remember vinyl?) followed. They proved that when you bring poetry to people the response is phenomenal.

The Poetry Virgins are living proof of this.

But why poetry and why Virgins ? Someone said that real examples of either are so rare as to put them on the endangered species list. Well, poetry because ..... it is. And Virgins ? Some of the women in The Poetry Virgins had never read poetry aloud before and typically, added humour to first night nerves. They continue to make every performance a first time in the best possible way.

Bringing poetry to life is a talent in itself. Keeping it alive and kicking is an art. The Poetry Virgins have been practising this art all over the North East for five years, in pubs, in clubs, in bars, and even in draughty towers. It is partly what they read: fresh approaches to well tried themes, poems, old and new. It is partly the way they read it: everyone knows that they are enjoying themselves and the pleasure is infectious.

And yes, most of the poems involve women's lives and experience. But you can forget the Hannah with a banner soap box feminists and the over serious polemic of early feminism: we are talking about the nitty gritty day to day living of our lives. Feminism twenty and thirty years ago suffered because it involved a language which was not our own: we were invaded by American Feminism and its' glossy and well-heeled jargon. But Rosie the Riveter said 'Feminist ? Of course I'm a feminist, I'm female.'
The language of the Poetry Virgins is one we understand, it's down to earth and witty, whether talking about children or parents or poverty or dreams. The canvas of the poetry is as wide as life experience. The material is always being updated and anyone is welcome to offer their works and have the delight of hearing it read aloud in public.

One of the strongest elements is humour and it was well said that humour can persuade people to consider another point of view where preaching and polemic fail dismally. Imagine a serious play about a right-wing facist bigot living in entrenched poverty with a wheelchair bound wife: we'd watch and feel awful and helpless. Put the same situation comically and we have 'In Sickness And In Health', which makes all the right points about old age and disability. Which is more memorable and which makes us care?

This collection ranges from thoughts on Tressy Dolls to dressing up and dreams of murder. The vast and complex interior world of modern day women, free to do anything as long as health and money and children and families permit. The women in this book are the strong women of Marge Piercy's poem:

'.....standing
on tiptoe and lifting a barbell
while trying to sing Boris Godunov'

There is no typical Poetry Virgins' audience just as there is no typical Poetry Virgins' poem. Teenagers, young women, old women, fathers, boyfriends, grandparents: everyone will find something here to stimulate and entertain them and maybe just set them thinking on a new track.

Enjoy !

Fiona Cooper

Contents

children

Only One Biscuit

I'll only have one biscuit,
I've put on so much weight..,
I've got to watch it.
what was I saying?
oh yes
I wonder if he wants a sleep yet
did you find that,
after you had the baby,
you were,... you know, sort of
oh god he's after that plant again,
sort of tired and
Not the plant!
lost concentration a bit?

well just one more, they are very nice
Tescos? I knew it!
he's going to smear biscuit on that new cushion cover..
what was I saying?
oh yes, concentration...
were you? I mean did you..? lose it, I mean?
the cushion cover, oh no!
I'm awfully sorry about the cushion cover, ha ha,
you know what it's like.
Give the biscuit to Mummy, there's a good boy,
No you can't have another
he can't be hungry he's not eating them
See? I have to finish up the bits.

no thanks, I'll finish his bits.
now where were we?
oh yes, I was thinking
he is definitely looking sleepy now
that something happens to your brain, when you have one.
Yes Mummy'll take you home soon, promise...
did you find that?
oh no, I can smell something...
I'm sorry, what did you say...?

Ellen Phethean

Naming of Parts, Too

is Freddie a boy ?
yes, he's got a penis hasn' he.
you're a woman, you haven't got one.
girls don't have them,
I've got a 'gina
and a clitris
and I can have a baby in my tummy
cam' I ?
when I was a baby I was in my mummy's tummy
wasn' I ?
an I drank milk from my mummy's breasts
boys don't have babies in their tummies,
don't they not ?
look! that's my gina !

Ellen Phethean

Tressy

shall I compare thee to a summer's day ?
thou art more plastic and yet more enduring
sweet maid, sure made to last a lifetime's play
the sun may shine but you are more alluring.
Tressy, keyhole secret of your silk
and golden locks, with wardrobes bursting ope
pert pouting breasts that ne'er shed mother's milk
possession each small girl's abiding hope.
your moulded sex will never show it's age
yet fashion lasts too short for parent's purse
with multi outfits set to strut the stage
your Tressy culture all young minds immerse

so long as girls love dolls, and cherish dreams
so long will men devise more dolly schemes.

Ellen Phethean

Big Mark

she says
I don't like school
I don't like Big Mark

he knocked my head
against the apparatus
then stole my scarf
left it hanging up the roof
I cried, but then I chased him
he hates kissing
he runs when you kiss him

he says girls are stupid
and pokes me in assembly
he says I'm ugly
I don't care
I'm stronger than him
I can run faster

he looks at girls' knickers
today I'll wear trousers
and with my gang
Kelly and Sam
we'll sit on him
and kiss him
because he hates kissing

anyway, I got him today
I stole his pencil
and scribbled on his book
you've told me not to write on books
but this is different
because you also said
stick up for yourself
well, I am

but I'm worried
about what will happen
tomorrow

tired of Big Mark
tired of running

Julia Darling

Inventions

Owen Maclaren, a caring, thoughtful man
went to collect his grandprogeny one day,
and was struck by the "transport problem",
oh yes - there were pushchairs and collapsible carrycots,
I mean, this is the 60's we're talking about

but they were heavy, man, and cumbersome.
Owen Maclaren, that enlightened, inventive man
had a vision:
a deckchair on wheels which folded
in a single-handed action and hooked over the arm
and lighter than the baby you held in the other

and of course, Owen Maclaren had a big advantage
he was a trained aeronautical engineer (retired)
he helped design Spitfire undercarriages during the war
so - naturally - he understood the requirements of
Lightweight, Load Bearing, Folding Structures

so there you are,
all of us who push our children around in
Lightweight, Load Bearing, Folding Structures,
just spare a thought for Owen 'Buggyman' Maclaren.
where would we be without him, or them?
stuck at home, unable to negotiate public transport

imagine !
now we can travel,
take up our opportunities
go to college
and become inventors
so we can turn weapons
into liberating household objects

Ellen Phethean

Crabbing

skulling a safe boat
holding a string, tied round a bone
catching crabs

small useless crabs
to hold nervously
between thumb and forefinger
then drop in the old red bucket
anchored by a bare toe

the sky touches my head
and the harbour sings
sail rattling songs

girls on the quayside
are stalking a different type
of mollusk
I am nearly too old
for this pointless pastime

soon the swell will rise
and the sweet singing become complicated
I will empty out the crabs
let them clatter down the slipway
tumbling over themselves
to reach home

until
the last crab settles sideways
into the waters
its' pin eyes goggling
safe in the shell
that hard exterior
sheltering such a fragile creature
within

Julia Darling

The Three Rs

WHAT ARE THREE TIMES SEVEN ! ?
I was petrified
NINE TIMES EIGHT ! ?
Mental Arithmetic
RECITE THE ELEVEN TIMES TABLE
reliable as Pavlov's dogs
Fridays brought sweaty   mental blocks
my peace of mind in
FRACTIONS
even now
WHAT'S SEVENTEEN PERCENT VAT ON TWENTY THREE
POUNDS ?
such questions
A THREE PERCENT PAYRISE ON EIGHT THOUSAND ?
conjure up the same sick swimminess

PRIME
or round
SQUARE ROOT
or quantum leap
number magic
nearly killed at birth
NOTHING TALLIES
Friday's test
eleven plus
cse maths
I never got
THE DECIMAL POINT
nor learnt the golden
slide rule

I'm reconciled with figures
now I'm
FORTY

they retain a mysterious
GEOMETRY
like my calculator
which pleases me

but I see my child starting
on the math's path
I start to feel the rising panic
adding or taking away
long division or multiplication

what are the
PROBABILITIES
for him ?

Ellen Phethean

Veni Video Vici

Teenage Mutant Ninja Violence, Turtles with a Shelf Life
He-Man, She-Angry
Thunder Cats, Thunderbirds are Go!

She-Pretty, He-Strong,
My Little Pony and Trap,
Insidious, In videos
Goodies and Baddies, Muscles and Curves
Who Cares Bears?

SUPER-SEXIST-RACIST-HOMOPHOBIC-IDEOLOGY
If you say it loud enough it really is infectious...
Honey I Brainwashed the Kids!

101 Damnations - We're the Dumbos...
Walt Disney is Not a Comrade

Ellen Phethean

teenagers

Janet

you and I we look good with our new trouser suits
you got the flares, mine has a waistcoat
you live near the station, we like swearing and singing
you come down my house, we make plans and we whisper
we've got them all nervous in our difficult phase

chewing gum, playing those dullbeat records
eyelids like letterboxes, heavy with shadow
at the youth club we make up our own dances
and at night in my bed, I listen past the voices
the vowels of the wealthy. I listen for trains.

the tourists have complained about me and you
the music, our faces, cracked hard with make up
pop up at the windows when they take their photos
we are the mosquitoes who buzz round the cattle
the lazy fat tourists, the boys in their gowns

we got dressed up on Saturday, in lipstick and false nails
we could see the headmaster from the drawing room window
SILLY OLD SOD....we jeered and drank all the sherry
talked in French accents
went hanging around the knotted old buildings
you wrote fuck on a sixteenth century fountain

we whistled at scholars, heads hung and dark blushing
then went to the library, sat in the classics
it was damp and smelt funny, just paper and latin
we could hear all this music, choirboys in the chapel
it was really divine, the tourists were weeping

we got out the varnish, wrote on the bible
WE ARE THE VANDALS
WE WERE HERE

Julia Darling

You're A Woman Now

Wobbly as not set jelly
refusing to firm up
in the mould

bouncing off my mother
a solid rubber ball

moods fragile and dark
as roofing slate

wrapped in unreliable anatomy
undercooked fried eggs
and an early wild cherry

staring uncertain
at the little rusty mark
that won't go away

suddenly trussed
an invalid
bandaged in feminine hygiene

sitting fully clothed
on a hot beach
lurking with my woman's secret

Ellen Phethean

Esther

when we were fourteen we nicked off
and jumped on a London bus
we went to Kings Cross and hung about
but no-one corrupted us

Julia Darling

God

As a child I hated God
star of school murals
and morning assemblies
mysterious bearded fancy dresser
electric fingertipped
who pointed and knew
God divined
the hatted parents
at sports day
beamed up ballot box contents
from polling booths
kept count
on the holy scoreboard of the firmaments
no escaping
God's Great Love, enveloping
brownies with properly cleaned teeth
girls who knew their hymn numbers
& tell tale tits
He laser beamed inner thoughts

is nothing sacred ? I cried

awed by the absurdity
angered by the omnipresent
punitive peeping judge
of playground
bathroom
and my head

I finally decided
not to believe in "Him"
I didn't need
a male tory dentist
spying on my life

Ellen Phethean

Thrift and Gorse

Phil and Dorothy
the teachers,
our holiday neighbours
every year

Phil wore red nail varnish
laughing, she chain smoked
plump Dorothy
northern and bronchial
laughed and coughed

Phil contained
in lambswool and ski pants
tweedy Dorothy
spilling over at the edges
a friendly gap between her teeth
it whistled now and again

unlike anyone else
wise oracles
the caravan in a cow field
commentators on the families
that holidayed
every year

as a monkey booted tomboy
invited to their caravan
to be taken seriously
I was interrogated
about sexual secrets
and school achievements
prompted and probed by their thorough eyes
I confessed

later in my twenties
they confided I had "turned out alright"
measured
on some moral scale
and found satisfactory

in their mobile home that never moved
solid cornish features
looked out for every year
like thrift and gorse

Ellen Phethean

Dances

mother, why do you dress me as an old woman ?
you rake my hair and put me in dangerous shoes
stick diamond twigs to my breast
and leave me at dances where I will look
ridiculous
the hostess does not look after me
I must talk to boys in paper suits
they wait by the pastry boats
and cannot kiss a girl without dribbling
my underwear aches
like you I am not the coupling type

twenty years later I have creeping regrets
thinking of those insubstantial boys
the alimony payments
the large castle attics
I could have disappeared in
their quiet asylums

how foolish I was to have scowled
and refused their vol au vents

mother you were absolutely right

Julia Darling

relationships

Foreign

foreign stations, foreign towns
the smell of foreign eiderdowns
the brittle toast, the bottled beer
foreign girls with foreign hair
foreign tickets, foreign trees
mosquito bites on both my knees
foreign eggs and foreign forks
foreign flowers on foreign stalks
foreign dust blows down the street
sitting on a foreign seat
listening to a foreign siren
as did Shelley, Keats and Byron
others came, my old art teacher
Violet and her girlfriend Vita
writing poems sat in bars
on beaches under foreign stars
wearing foreign trousers, kissing
maybe going foreign fishing

but you and I read english books
and exchange meaningful looks
we arch our eyebrows in distaste
at foreign men with bulging waists
we wait, we lie together sleeping
while foreign cars keep foreign bleeping
we murmur softly as we can
rubbing cream on slight suntans

and later in a foreign room
in the foreign shuttered gloom
filled with foreign things to eat
we laugh beneath a foreign sheet

make british vows in foreign places
and stroke each others foreign faces

Julia Darling

Forecasting

he was a viking in his forties
tyne after tyne I said, don't dogger me
just don't dogger me...but he fishered
me a single parent with no german bite
I came to like his humber
and eventually thames towards him
dover and dover
we caught the white of each other's lundy
throwing all faeroes into the fast net
deep in our Irish sea
rockallin' and dancin' the mallin
those were the hebrides years
until Cromarty...
how I wish Cromarty had not met my viking
still only forty....we tyned and doggered
until my fisher ran out
and he got his german bite alright
humbering halfway up the Thames
waves dover him
his white in the dark lundy
faeroes swept from the fastnet

I have drunk the Irish Sea
hearing him, calling through ships
rock.....all
mall...........in
CROMARTY

thanks Cromarty....I hope you sink
someday

Julia Darling

Meeting

meeting you reminds me
of that time I poured boiling water
on ants in the Isle of Wight
after a while
I felt really sick

Julia Darling

Long Conversation

first the babies...
remember that time they were sick
and you and I, drowning in the smell of vomit
laughed because
it was so awful
it couldn't get worse

then the husbands
unlaughing unfaithful unfriendly
fuelling our mutual despair
locked in our fetid backrooms
we sent out flares
hoping the other would hear

at the mother and toddler group
we sneered and tried to get
the best biscuits, refusing
to idolise our children
we played with the pastry
and talked of mistakes

when the husbands left
we raged on each other's doorsteps
packed picnic baskets
together we made a crowd
at the park, the museum
we worked hard that year

our new definition
was not in the catalogue
we got drunk in the kitchen
knew fear, faced aloneness
and never lied
about smacking our children

it's not over
ours is a long conversation
now uncluttered with husbands
our faces seem stronger
the future much longer
all our colours are richer and deeper

Julia Darling

23

Bananas

She said, "Madam, please don't squash the bananas."
Ooh, I feel so angry, looking back at it, her treating me like a
five-year-old. Well I wasn't going to take that bunch she held
up. All green they were. Harry doesn't like green bananas,
never has. I remember, just after the war, standing in the ration
queue and the word came down the line - "They've got
bananas one per ration book. " I'd never had a banana, before -
couldn't afford them before the war and there certainly wasn't
any foreign stuff around during it - except for Yankee chewing
gum, but that's another story.
I remember Harry's face when he first tasted bananas; his grin
was like one. He's loved them ever since.
So it was important you see, him being in hospital, that I got a
bunch not too ripe, just on the turn. They don't feed them
properly in hospital, especially not when they're old and
pernickety like Harry.
Ooh, I was flustered when she said that. I needed to get to the
bus stop sharpish because the hospital bus is only once an hour.
I'd already got the essentials - writing pad and envelopes so he
can write to the grand bairns, bar of Fry's chocolate, Steredent.
Then I saw those bananas and I knew he'd love them. That
bright yellow - they'd really put some sunshine on his bedside
table. They're a bit expensive this time of year and the pension
wouldn't really stretch to it.
I can never think of what to say when the young 'uns are sarky
like that. Afterwards I can. Who does she think she is - just a
market trader. Any other time I'd have walked away.
But I needed to see Harry's face light up, just one more time.

Jean Seagroatt

Shagging

you meet someone you half know at a crowded bar
she lurches like a tree
and smiles, quite cynically......
she says ......who you shagging then?
I say........last July was the last straw
she says ...aye?
what about you? I say laughing
two years......she says.......
this is when I realise
times have changed

Julia Darling

Open Window

open the window for a while
the weeds in the backyard grow tall
and though black silk flaps against the pane
I can still see the garden wall

open the window, untidy the dust
for the trees are shadowy dancers
we'll dance on the carpet, the red raggy carpet
and you, you can still be my partner

Julia Darling

politics

Reminiscence

(on the occasion of my mother visiting Beamish Museum)

you were frightened
by the recreated co-operative store
at the living museum

you said,
imagine it
the whole of Tescos recreated
each tin and free offer
the music, the carrier bags
even the shoplifters

and what if they took you
on trips down a lifesize replica
of the M1, in a coach
and you too old to stop them

if they took your teapots
and put them in rooms
that smelt of the Thatcher years

poll tax bills lying on the doormat
the door locked twenty times
news of the war on television

those were the days
of the entrepreneur
says the guided talk
marvelling at the antiquity
of your ansafone

far better, you said
to forget...

and shivered

Julia Darling

Poverty

you don't see it
it's packed out of town
in houses with no furniture
waiting for cheques that come by post
handed out by the invisible
watched over by shadows
kept in files and case histories
you know it by its' bus routes
by what the shops are selling
by lettuce leaves, by mushroom stalks
by bargains and poundstretchers
betting shops and lotteries
by well dressed children that cry
by how many seagulls are out looking for food
and how many dogs are out leadless
too many hairdressers
and not enough cafes
by out of date community posters
by social clubs with locks
broken windows with bars
and policeman who stay in their cars
by murals gone faded
sofa beds costing only forty five quid
and people who are friendly
but on their own
who talk as if they know you
and are used to not being heard
by women with babies and no prams
and the men in the park who smoke
and watch toddlers
by women with prams and no babies

you know it by its' silence
voicelessness
poverty

Julia Darling

River Mouth

choppy mouth, what do you say ?
tidal talk, sucking on toothless gums
the cranes, the structure gone
leaving sunken banks
the chink and grind of enamel
replaced with a false set
for show only, no power to chew

spit head mouth, spewing
foul odours, stained
with a lifetime's passage
of coal pit tar and human waste
in and out, up and down
the gullet of the Tyne
with a metallic aftertaste

open mouthed you gape
at new developments
pink imposing quayside courts
warehouse upgrades to luxury flats
tall ships race for fun
history redundant
your ebb and flow
museum of the leisured

silent mouth, tongue tied
aching bridge work
banks shored up
smart slabs and railings
overlaid and even-edged
sit uncomfortable
rubbing raw jaw bones

Ellen Phethean

Metroland

Artifice
the art of surface
what you see
is not what you get

see through lifts
glass reflecting
mirror exit doors
camouflaged

greek taverna
one week
country and western
the next
Dickens style marble effect
Pallas Athene plywood pillars
living plants that look plastic

peep behind glass
reflecting
on breeze blocks
concrete
the car parks
the people who aren't here

Ellen Phethean

Christopher Isherwood

The night before Christopher Isherwood died, I was at home
drinking coffee.
At the time I didn't know where Christopher Isherwood was.
I didn't know what he'd been doing since writing that book
which they based the film Cabaret on.
In fact, I hadn't thought about Christopher Isherwood for ages.
Then, between sips, it suddenly came to me.
Whatever happened to Christopher Isherwood ?
The next day he was dead.

He's the only person I've ever killed personally, but I know
other people who've done it quite a few times.
Actually, it was a friend of mine who finished off Greta Garbo.
And it was my friend Tessa who killed Simone de Beauvoir.
It's funny though, I often wonder what happened to Margaret
Thatcher.
I say to people - whatever happened to Margaret Thatcher ?
Ask yourself.

Jane Barnett

Pravda

I was listening to the radio the other morning,
half awake
when I heard this item
about the collapse of communism

everything was being affected, they said
even Pravda
the newspaper
Pravda, they said, meant "truth" in Russian
so what was happening to Pravda ?
the interviewer asked

oh yes,
the man replied
it disappeared for a week
it changed
they might not call it Pravda anymore

was this a sign
the interviewer asked
that Russian newspapers
would now print
the real truth ?

Ellen Phethean

Sacred Cow

at fourteen she was raped
a shadowy figure
someone she knew
or liked?

at fourteen she was abused
stalked, pursued,
exposed in court
a law she knew or trusted ?

at fourteen she was a sacred cow
constitutionally quickened
single parent and bastard,
two poor children

not the church, not the state, women must decide their fate

Ellen Phethean

Avoidance

I am filtering water and washing apples
examining eggs and looking closely at their smooth shells
for something inexplicable, a clue
slicing broccoli with distrust
frying sausages with a suicidal sneer
snifting milk and only using the hearts of lettuce

is this normal ?

to gulp pints of lager evading images
of huge vats of bubbling chemical
shutting my eyes when I eat a prawn
while used condoms and cleaning detergents
swim before my eyes

does everyone do this ?

on country walks I smell crop spray
and shake my head at blackberries
I smoke to take my mind off things
wonder why organic vegetables are more expensive
and buy eggs delivered by tortured chickens

I don't know why I believe in marmite
but I do...

even a malteser looks suspicious
a fish positively malevolent
stuck with dubious sandwiches
and vitamin pills
we wait, with shallow breaths
for nourishment.

Julia Darling

health

Evacuation Of Remaining Products

Grey mashed potato clouds, lumpy and cold
whippety wind trees bare, save for plastic shreds
a blow in the park, stinging with rain
a mucous sick baby crying and snotty
a smashed car window
lads running down wet back lanes
dead-give-away cassettes rattling in pockets

but the litmus paper turned pink
marking your beginning
a bright spot
in an otherwise cold northern sunday

I was looking forward to small hands
little perfection of crescent moons
nails too impossibly tiny to trim with scissors
translucent fingers
I would have marvelled at their miniature completeness
and brushed their softness with my lips
mesmerised by their graceful suddenness

I will not have that satisfaction
you were a cluster of potential, never more.
Too many deaths, too many euphemisms
each death painful
with echoes of the last, of lost wishes

The white overalled team
so cleanly kind
cannot cut away
the remaining products
of experience

Ellen Phethean

Amazon

my love
do you still fancy me ?

will you
kiss every inch of me,
blissfully ?

caress
all the flesh of me ?

undress
me, greedily ?

touch
me as much
as you did
before they got rid
of my breast ?

It had to be done. I hadn't a choice.
I felt like a puppet without my own voice.
Others knew better. All that advice
Was my body my own ? I had to think twice.

well,
it was hell.

only a woman can know what I mean,
a living nightmare, not merely a dream.

my chest
feels undressed.

I feel lopsided. Half of me's gone.
I feel everyone knows I've got only one...

am I unattractive ? I'm frightened. So blue.
Am I still the best thing that's happened to you ?

will you suggest
single beds ?
detest my bare skin ?

where do we begin ?

I'm the same as before, just a little bit less
what are you thinking, my love ?
don't leave me to guess

I'm an Amazon now.

Moira McLean

Jekyll and Hyde

Jelly bowelled
a ripe seed about to burst
blown up full and hollow
clumsy, cumbersome, muddled
I mistime, mistake
hand eye co-ordination
gone for a period

a wild beast on the prowl
an irritated lion, roaring
a bad tempered camel, spitting
lashing out
with my tongue
out of control

a foundering wreck
weeping, apologising
shivering cold
sunk into arctic depression
emotionally adrift
on an oceanic sea of sadness

released by
the intimate deep red sign,
familiar painful tenderness
strangely comforting
the switchback ride is over

for another month

Ellen Phethean

Asthma

wheezy sneezy lemon squeezy
asthma inhaler puffing huffing
itchy eyes itchy throat
dripping nose pollen count
nasal passage coughing cough
bronchial spasms feeling rough
irritated tissues breathing tight
watery lids and wakeful nights
heaving chest panting breaths
run upstairs sit down to rest
doing it deep, controlled and slow
shake inhaler, go go go
insert tube,
press...

suck - - -

hold

Ellen Phethean

The Body (a found poem)

the body contains enough lime

to whitewash a hen coop

enough iron to make a nail

enough phosphorus to tip two thousand matches

enough sulphur to rid a dog of fleas

enough potash to blow up a toy car

enough sugar to sweeten six cups of tea

enough fat to make seven bars of soap

if you like that sort of thing

Julia Darling

Safe In Our Hands

Safe in your hands ?
You mean like the NHS and Margaret Thatcher safe ?

The doctor asks me personal questions,
like how much do I drink and how often ?
I mentally calculate, then lie
that's too much, she says
for a healthy diet

but doctor, I think,
I'm not safe in my hands
I eat too much rubbish,
I stay up too late and get tired
I avoid exercise
I watch too much television
I read Blacks Medical Dictionary
(doctors have told me about this before)
that's how I know I'm an Amyl -
an alcohol radical
I shout about feminism after a few drinks

Just be sensible, she says,
looking at me, smiling
there's nothing really wrong
nothing sensible habits wouldn't put right.
and I wonder
if we share the same definition of sensible,
the doctor, the NHS Managers, the Government
and me?

Ellen Phethean

writing

Apology

I'm not sure I should read this one...
it's not really finished.........the germ of an idea, really
anyway - it's only short!
I'm not that satisfied with it, actually
needs more work on it, I just scribbled it down yesterday.
I had a headache when I wrote it, that's why it's not
very...perhaps I won't read it
I know you won't like it...
well alright - here goes

Ellen Phethean

Writing Group

Fancy that!   I'm a poet and I didn't even know it.

anyone can write she said, and you do, every day -
shopping lists, notes to the teacher, letters to relatives
oh yes, but that isn't poetry
any fool can do that.

Wordsworth didn't write shopping lists,
Shakespeare didn't send notes to his child's teacher,
exactly! she said...exactly what I'm not sure...

just start with short pieces, she said, what comes into your
head,
relax and think about this morning - what did you do ? she said,

well, what a stupid...I woke up and got out of bed... I mean !
yes, but how exactly, tell us, we want to hear
about how you felt, what you thought - make it clear.

well I have to admit, when we read them out
we'd all got up, made breakfast, but each one
was about us being so different, as well as the same,
about all of us.

It's not easy - this poetry's not about daffodils
...what rhymes with daffodils...?

I think I should have used another word...

Ellen Phethean

Making Words

I find making words
can't be done to order
I have to be in the mood

the mood can strike
but I can't find my pen
worse, I have my pen
but no mood
empty white sheets
seem suddenly unappealing

its much more fun
when I know I should be doing
something else
it's no fun if I try too hard
and fatal if I pretend.

impossible
in small cornish cottages,
overcrowded tyneside flats
when relatives
are staying

a watched kettle never boils

although I 've done it
in unusual places
on a cliff top, in the bath
while I'm ironing

making words on my own
can be lonely
making words with others
is more friendly,

and making words between the covers
is the consummate experience

Ellen Phethean

Sylvia

I wandered lonely as a 1lb of potatoes, 2lbs onions,
sprouts, bread

My love is like a red, red rose, and don't forget:
Phone school, cancel milk friday, write   Susan
Send dad's birthday card

To be or not to be
collecting kids from school today and
remember John to dentist 5.00

Season of mists and mellow fruitfulness
Sylvia 221 2341
dentist 273 6617
Sylvia 9.30 Dog and Parrot
Who is Sylvia? What is she...?

J. Smith, John Smith, John H. Smith, John Harold Smith,
Hi, JH here...
John! Have you been using my writing pad again ?

Hubble, bubble, toil and trouble
Onions, sprouts and kids from school
Onions, sprouts, kids from school
Silver dentist, dog and parrot,
write milk, cancel carrot,
kids from school and birthday card
Tell me, why is writing hard ?

Ellen Phethean

Poem Of man With Dictaphone

Hello Susan
take this down please
date it last Friday
it's urgent to Pisansky
P S no P E Z
damn his name
it's on the letterhead
address blah blah
it's on the file
dear bob etc
you know the style
re the matter
check the matter Susan
end heading, refer to latter
it's in hand,
at next opportunity
will discuss and
get back a.s.a.p.
you know the sort
of thing stop
letter ends   yours
blah blah etcetera
oh pp it would you
thanks and don't forget
it's semi skimmed in my coffee, Sue
poem ends

Ellen Phethean

Sonnet of Audio Typist

A besuited man there was who couldn't spell
to save his life. Poor literary style
did not worry him or give him hell
no nothing stopped him climbing up the pile.
His failures never reached the public's eye
a guardian angel hovering with good will
would monitor his errors, none slipped by
her expert eye, and with her typing skill
she'd listen to his dictaphonic scramble
decipher and unscramble it and better
rework it and by trimming, cut the ramble
and finally produce a perfect letter.

I know, because that skilful she was me
and I earnt less than half of his fat fee.

Ellen Phethean

Poetry Virgin

Leaning on my ironing board
scribbling notes for another poem
making rhymes out of recipes
tagging along with the mothers and dawdlers
rehearsing verses
scrubbing the fridge
scouring my mental elements

worrying
about unironed poems
uncooked phrases
unwatered ideas
and
good-enough
writing.

Ellen Phethean

The Writer Dreams of Leaving Work

I will grow a bark
and bud-clusters around myself at the start
of the new financial year.
I will grow little wings
and flap them in the toilets, damply, while
the telephone rings and suited men
beat about the bush.

I will become incomprehensible
and swim in the chlorinated municipal pool, naked,
in the lunch hour.
I will leave under a cloud,
disappear like a missing invoice,
become miscellaneous,
unaccountable.

Joan Johnston

Bald Poet's Head

oh poet, with your head so large and knowledgeable
oh huge man with your cabinets stuffed with books
ah, grand literati, with such solid flair
there's one thing I've got you haven't ...hair

Julia Darling

miscellany

Oh Madam

oh madam you are so opaque
your ringless smile a white light
and your eyes like glass dishes
I speak into your vortex
giddily, the sound all sucked away
you instruct...look as if you're listening
and smile like elastoplast

I want to tell you everything
that face, half therapist, half gynaecologist
is so receptive
instantly sympathetic
I will tell you everything

but you are bored, too quickly
packing your professional bag
turning the lights out
you lead the cameras away
to cover another
with that bright colour attention

oh madam
I told you everything
and now I fear you have forgotten
my story is all yesterday
while you are immortal
always perfect,

part of the crystal set

Julia Darling

Buying Cars

do not do what I have done
you'll end up lost on the cold M1
or stranded with your big end gone
do not do what I have done

don't trust men with MOTs
who offer Fiestas with guarantees
and never say thank you and never say please
while handing you over the grimy keys

of the shining Fiesta that shudders inside
it's really a Lada with bits on the side
a frankenstein, with it's ends untied
it's linings and bearings all tangled and fried

and when you return with a dying car
you'll find that Terry has gone to the bar
and Michael has gone off looking for scrap
and Gary says.... they'll phone you back

so zip up your jacket, hold up your chin
and unravel the mysteries of the engine within
study your manual, don't believe him
when he says he's adjusted your steering pin

no, don't believe Terry or Gary or Pete
who hide in the alleys behind every street
join the RAC or use your feet
and buy some spanners.....reet !

just don't do what I have done
there's nowhere so lonely as the cold M1
as the hard shoulder with your big end gone
do not do what I have done

Julia Darling

Stages of Drunkeness

I have been pickled now for 20 years now
starting with rum and coke...dark
like rooms I hid in, arms around shadows
pissed behind the sofa, illicit gulps
sophisticated and sordid
worth it for the words
rum and coke please
I'll have a rum and coke

the merrydown cider days were less stylish
gulped in public toilets sat on hard tiles
scratching my name with a compass point
waiting for my turn, my swig

not forgetting quiet sherry hours
alone in the garden shed with Q.C
it had a kind of ceremony, a holiness
everyone else was at church

then pub age, and bitter with pool
my pint glass heavy and satisfying
riding the beer froth before sinking
gracelessly on cue

next came love and vodka. in plastic tumblers
vodka on the carpet. in a flask
in bed. with orange. kisses that tasted
watery and sweet. open aired and inseparable
from vodka

as a communist I drank red wine
although I defected to beer
and became confused on real ale

it's been ten years now
of feminist lager, red stripes of Stella
run through my veins

they tell me Grey Street was once a river
it still is

I have wined on Thatcher
the world going by in its' agonies
while we drink our blurred refreshments

and now I'm running to Mexico
lemon and salt and a quick shot
tequilla, tequilla, one two three GO
I may well fall on an ice pick

after all this I still can't decide
if the world looks better sober

I hope you appreciate this sodden history
really just an aperitif
perhaps you too could make notes
on your own stages of drunkeness
and we can discuss them later
in the bar

                                        Julia Darling

Television

Hospitality measured in bottles
hair like pork crackling
face like cracked porcelain
hot studio one
with a cold audience
hours of waiting
seconds of rehearsal
all for one minute
of obscurity

                                        Ellen Phethean

Night Visitors

nocturnal Cornish creatures
disembowel my dustbin once again,
doughty paws tip over the metal bin
rake over the rubbish
spilling left overs all over

I weight the lid with granite
I wedge the bin
I wake in the early hours
listening in the dark to the clatter and bang
the mysterious snuffle, grunt, rustle and rummage
of those unseen night visitors
making swift work of my human stratagems...
can I hear laughter ?

surveying the strewn binbag innards
I sigh and try again,
the granite slabs, the wedging,
and this time a stretchy spider
hooked to the dustbin handles

next dustbin day the bin is all askew
but the lid stayed tight,
the doughty paws were defeated
by the stretchy spider,
a Pyrrhic victory.

Ellen Phethean

Life Begins at 40

I was a postwar 50's boom
what will you be ?
have you any inkling how many people there are
on earth,
my mother says
"Babies come when they want to"

Dear jelly baby
should I mention
nuclear global-warming
patriarchal multinational capitalism ?

lacking clairvoyancy
my heart is blind

your bodyheat home
shields you
from the graffiti
of life

for the moment

Ellen Phethean

Italian Shopping

somehow
by moving a toilet roll
I have dislodged the cap
on a bottle of toilet cleanser

it runs down the shampoo packets
noiselessly

I have no words for it
not even sorry
so I glide round to the fruit and veg
and stare at strange tomatoes
wonder at purple beans

pointing dumbly
I try to buy vinegar
she gives me flour

stupid in my grinning silence
indicating eggs
wishing I could talk
about the weather

Julia Darling

Disrespectful To Lakes

turning the corner
low gears growling with the slow
twist of the fell road
a tractor ahead
laughing
all the way to the corn field

another bloody epic scape
mountains scars and riggs
deep blue lakes
polished gorse
and organised brooks

I clamp my throat
not paying homage
to this unnatural postcard
it won't squeeze
one word of praise
from me

I will wince my way
along the national trust footpath
silently, withstanding
the sycophantic drawl
of the white middle aged rambler

saving words
for the greasy dust
of the city at sunset

Julia Darling

Birth Of A Mother

Pregnant
I wanted to laugh weep cry NO ! NO !
horrified tingling with anticipation
so many mixed feelings
foretelling mixed feelings to come

the elation always underridden
by a deep current
millenia weight
woman's condition
scared
vulnerable
ultimately responsible
for Life itself

How can I bear this ?
I am weak, unreliable
I resent my needs
where is my strong
independent single self ?
gone gone
never, ever single again
always thinking for two
I look at
women with children anew
with fascination
scanning faces for clues

finally comforted
I will find
my strong self
born in new form

an uneasy delivery
helpless at first
a slow learning
of the role
but still growing....

Ellen Phethean

Gladys' Last Attack

Gladys is planning her last attack
she has fought the corners of carpets long enough
tiger memories rustle behind curtains
her haunches spring like oiled caterpillars
she despises the domestic, is mad at this city life
the tin opener, the waiting

her of the wide feet and tangled hair
has forgotten her again
voices speak to Gladys on the ansafone
her fierce head furrs up with them
Gladys hurls paper across the room
catching the fluttering wings
with sharp jungle teeth

and at night dances alone on the scratched chairs
quick things dancing on the edges
of her wild green eyes

in this spiderless silence
Gladys plans her attack
on her, the old lion woman
who limps in, weary of the dangerous world
calling into the cavernous rooms
not knowing that Gladys waits
wild as a stalking leopard
about to stalk up the vertebrae
of her owner's shadow

Julia Darling

great women

Only Women

Because only women bleed,
are mothers,
need womens' refuges,
and have gynaecologists
have periods
scrapes
smears
coils
swabs,
caps
women's troubles
have PMT
have to sit down to piss
and never have enough toilets when they need them
have to pay VAT on tampax
and only women aren't in the cabinet

because only women can be dykes
and have a clitoris
(purely for pleasure, of course)
and fancy kd lang
and only women are wives,
mistresses,
girls,
feminists,
giggle,
gossip,
give birth,
turn bad
have their bits sewn up
have boobies
basoomies,
bristols,
breasts,
knockers
ad nauseam
but only women breastfeed
and have periods

because only women are wanton,
slags,
harridens,
vixens,
viragos,
amazons,
witches,
dumb blondes,
bits of fluff,
attractive brunettes
are described in numbers:
36,
24,
36

Because only women are women truck drivers
women taxi drivers
women bus drivers
are women drivers !
and have periods

because only women are princesses,
wicked stepmothers
fairy godmothers
principal boys
Brown Owl
Arkeyla
queens - well, maybe not,
thats a drag
are barmaids,
meter maids,
milk maids,
old maids,
dinner ladies,
Our Lady
mothers' little helpers
and know what clothes to dress the kids in every morning

because only women can bend over with their arms behind
their backs
and pick up a matchbox in their teeth
Is that right ?
yes, try it in the bar later

because only women have unsightly facial hair
wax their bikini line,
have bikini lines
have female intuition,
complain about Hennes adverts,
can't be the Pope,
or a vicar
know how to let their hair down,
get hysterical
and have periods

because only women have the menopause
what about the male menopause ?
not the same
tis
tisn't
we'll talk about it in the bar later

because only women have to wear the veil
and only women are unclean
(when they have their periods !)
and work two thirds of the worlds' working hours
for one tenth of it's income
and own less than one percent of the worlds' property
(and have periods !)

because only women are 'women writers',
women artists,
women musicians,
women playwrights
and because women-only is a dirty word

this is a women only event

Tessa Green & Ellen Phethean

Tartan Aunt

does everyone have a tartan aunt ?
a church stone of a woman
with a splendid bosom
and structural bodice
a cathedral of the parish ?

I still stomp with my fearsome aunt
craving her mission
she who loved so many dead men
who rolled with Robbie Burns
and became famous
for her lack of patience
with the living

who cares now
about the odd smells in her hallway
the disconcerting silver fish
slithering through her kitchen

she was mighty
even when plumped
on the pink pillow
of illness

our last stomp...

she forgot her shoes
I never mentioned this
although I saw her toes turn blue
in cold November street dirt

I preferred her tartan heart
rising up....flying over the spires

Julia Darling

Middle Child

Squeezed out,
you always felt squeezed out
by five surrounding siblings
by sharing
beds, food, clothes,
maternal interest

family gatherings
find you hurrying to the front door
the odd one
out, for a solitary walk
alone in the corner, reading

you felt squeezed
between husband and England
office and kitchen
your mind
pulling up and out
like a kite on apron strings
each tug back
sending you flying higher.

cutting ties
took you to french speaking Geneva
further, to America
the squeezing out now a pushing out
a leaving behind,
a Mayflowering
a spiritual journeying
never reaching middle age
you grow younger, horizons wider
the middle child regrets and resentments
diminish perspectives
on a family far distant

the world your oyster
the irritant grit
revealing opalescent qualities
a single pearl,
years in the forming

Ellen Phethean

Ordinary Woman

By day, she works in the shop.
Slicing ham off the bone.
Unpacking the cheese,
Worrying about kids and G.C.S.E's
And open cast mining
But how will it affect us.

Surely you don't need any more sprouts Miss Many
You're 78 man, you'll never eat them,
Please yourself you daft old bat.

Hoping the catalogue wife will forget today...
Fat chance of that.
Ding Dong Avon calling...
Somebody told me you'd died,
Oh well never mind, me purse is on the shelf.
Just like an ordinary woman.

By night it's tooty fruity,
Good golly miss molly you're looking jolly.
Me husband got two years
Never mind it could have been worse...
Could have been six months....ain't that a shame.

Spotted pink taffeta frocks swirl in time to great
balls of fire,
Eyes light up as the wanderer enters the scene.
She leaps and struts weaves and jumps
The golden girl, surrounded by golden girls
And as she walks home filled with passion and invincibility
She casually tosses a brick through the coal boards' window.
Just like an ordinary woman.

Karin Young

Carnival Queens

This is a cautionary tale about queens
about events that took place in a town by the sea
where every year the people made
a fantastic queen for the carnival parade
the moral is... if once you've felt gay
well, it's not very nice if it's taken away

anyway... the story I tell is one of rebellion
that happened, when after a thousand millenium
a certain mayor, both straight and mean
put a stop to having a carnival queen
put a stop to having a carnival queen

no-one could believe it, the women went pale
their mutterings became a wail
there were rumblings down the promenade
sounds of smashing glass in the old arcade
doors were opening, I smelt burning meat
heard muted growls and slippered feet
Karen Well-Be-Loved
(...... carnival queen in sixty-eight)
was crashing through her garden gate
with Anna Tilley, from nineteen forty two
(she was dressed as a mermaid and her escorts were blue)
There were suddenly hundreds of ex-queens in the square
even old Rita Jarvis had got out of her chair
they were spitting and cursing, stamping their feet
then they put Rita up in some kind of seat.....
(she was still in her nightie and her hair was in rollers,
she was piercing the air with a half knitted pullover)

they formed a circle and started to lurch
lead by Elsie who did the flowers in the church
and Freda MacIntosh who washes fish
(she was the queen in that terrible mist)
WHAT DO WE SAY ? and angry eyes met
that once had watered through sequinned net,
RATHER A CARNIVAL QUEEN THAN A BRIDE !
yelled a miserably married queen from the side
I RECKON THAT LITTLE SIT ON A THRONE
WAS THE NICEST REST I'VE EVER KNOWN...
WHAT ARE WE? QUEENS !
and they began to frolic

and drinks appeared, all alcoholic,
all these queens, through lunch and tea
danced and whirled obliviously,
they threw off their shoes, let down their hair
danced in the shops, danced everywhere
and all they muttered, swore and screamed was
BRING US THIS YEAR'S CARNIVAL QUEEN ! !

I was there, I saw it all
those carnival queens just had a ball!

then the mayor appeared, dressed in suit
and everyone hushed, with one final hoot

LADIES, he said, OR SHOULD I SAY QUEENS
WE HAVE REACHED A DECISION, YOU KNOW WHAT
THAT MEANS
YOU CAN'T, YOU MUSTN'T, YOU SHOULDN'T, YOU
WON'T...

Rita hissed...OH NO YOU DON'T

HERE'S SOME FLOWERS, yelled Mrs Savage
throwing down some sprouting cabbage
and for your veil, a polishing rag
your dress, a billowing black dustbin bag
we've dressed each other, now we'll dress you
you ain't worth a tinsel, or a cheap tu-tu
a saucepan landed on his head
his float was an unmade single bed
they sprinkled ajax in his hair
he didn't stop them, he didn't dare...

Rita raised a triumphant lavatory brush
inspiring a deep respectful hush
WE ARE ALL QUEENS, she said with vigour
NEVER MIND OUR CLOTHES AND FIGURES
AND IF WE WANT TO WEAR PINK NETTING
WE'LL DO IT ALL YEAR ROUND, IN ANY SETTING
ONCE IN A LIFETIME JUST WASN'T ENOUGH
and everyone nodded and everyone laughed

we carried on frolicking, we forgot the mayor
we frolicked all night, we didn't care

I've never forgotten Rita's words
the things I saw, the things I heard

you see...I picked a spot
and when it bled
my blood was royal blue, not crimson red
my blood was blue, and I am sure
that yours is too.

Julia Darling

A Woman's Art Is Never Done

I know a woman
who hangs up her washing
carefully selected by colour
for the pleasure it gives her

I know another
who has a bath with her children
every time the going gets tough
for the fun of it

I know another, my mother
who would sing loudly
when her children nagged her

I know a woman
who sniffs her bare arms
in summer
because she likes the smell of them

I know a woman
who always eats peas
because she needs green
on her white plates

I know a woman
who buys flowers for herself
and enjoys feeling
wickedly extravagant

I know a woman
who arranges her milk bottles
symmetrically on the doorstep
because it puts pattern in her life

I am a woman
who writes poetry in my head
while I'm ironing
I write
for all the ironed, pressed, scrubbed, cooked, sung
women's moments
because a woman's art is never done.

Ellen Phethean

Modern Goddess

goddesses have changed hands
cathedrals are full of their spaces
churches squeak with their pips
when they rise it is from cereal packets
they are embossed on margarine

I found a goddess in Yates Wine Lodge
she spat and sang and had royal hair
my aunt was a goddess, although vain
badly dressed and demented,
silver fish swam in her flour bins

my youngest child is also a goddess
she has told me often about the times
men with horns ransacked her villages
I agree with her..it was dreadful
what they did to goats

sometimes I see them, goddesses
in the swimming baths, or at coffee mornings
but I have never seen one on the television

you will know them by their stone eyes
and weighted walk
goddesses will use silence loudly
and remember this

you never see a goddess with a handbag

do not be rude to goddesses
even in supermarkets or waiting rooms
they know all about you

and unlike gods they are modern
tireless and undead
real as teabags

Julia Darling

Acknowledgements

We'd like to thank the following:

Christine Alderson
Angela Lamb
Bev Robinson
Northern Arts
Gateshead Libraries and Arts
Fiona Cooper
Keith Morris
Joyce Morris
Bobby
Harry
Freddie
Florrie
Scarlet
Josie
Scamp
Eve Hardwick
and our audiences and the women
who have sent us poems.

Biographies

Julia Darling

Broadcasting - Tyne Tees TV and Fem FM. Published by Women's Press, Hybrid Press. "Small Beauties" a collection os poems published by Newcastle Libraries. Plays commisioned by Live Theatre, Tyne Wear T.I.E., Crucible T.I.E. Sheffield, Northumberland Youth Theatre, Chopwell Drama Group, C.P. Taylor Bursary 1991, Quondam Arts Trust.

Ellen Phethean

Actor/Writer with the Women's Theatre Group, M6 Theatre, NE1 Theatre, TyneWear T.I.E., Bruvvers, Sugar & Spikes, Major Diversion. Broadcast by Fem FM.

Jane Barnett

Formerly worked as an actor and musician, currently a freelance sound recordist all over the world.

Karin Young

Actor/Writer with NE1 Theatre. Writer and Director with My Aunt Fanny Films. Commissioned by Live Theatre.

Tessa Green

Singer/Songwriter, worked with local musicians - The Hotpoints, Bitsa Band, Sugar & Spikes. Currently working with Tessa & Charlie.

Joan Johnston

Writing steadily since 1985, she has been published by The Page and W.E.A. She was 2nd in the Gateshead Short Story Competition last year, this year she won it!

Moira McLean

Originally a nurse and midwife, now a poetry and prose writer, published locally and by Sheba Press, she has had a play included in the National Extension College 'Reading Women Writers' poetry course.

Jean Seagroatt

A member of Future Tense, a women's writing and performing group, she won 2nd prize in the Durham Lit Fest Poetry Competition this year, and has been published by The Page.

Fiona Cooper

Author of five novels, Rotary Spokes, Heartbreak on The High Sierra, Jay Loves Lucy, Not The Swiss Family Robinson and The Empress of The Seven Oceans. She has written numerous short stories and journalistic satires and lives on Tyneside.

Poetry Virgins 1992. Left to right:
Ellen Phethean, Kay Hepplewhite, Charlie Hardwick,
Julia Darling, Fiona MacPherson.

Published by

DIAMOND TWIG

5, Bentinck Road, Newcastle upon Tyne NE4 6UT
Printed by Bailes Fastprint, Houghton Le Spring
September 1992